Dear red fan parrot:

Where did you get that funny hat?

I'm not wearing a hat. Those are my feathers. When I'm frightened, I fan them out to make me look larger and more intimidating.

Dear harpy eagle:

And why are *your* feathers sticking out?

It's not because I'm scared — I'm one of the largest, fiercest birds in the world. Those feathers help me hear by directing sound to my ears.

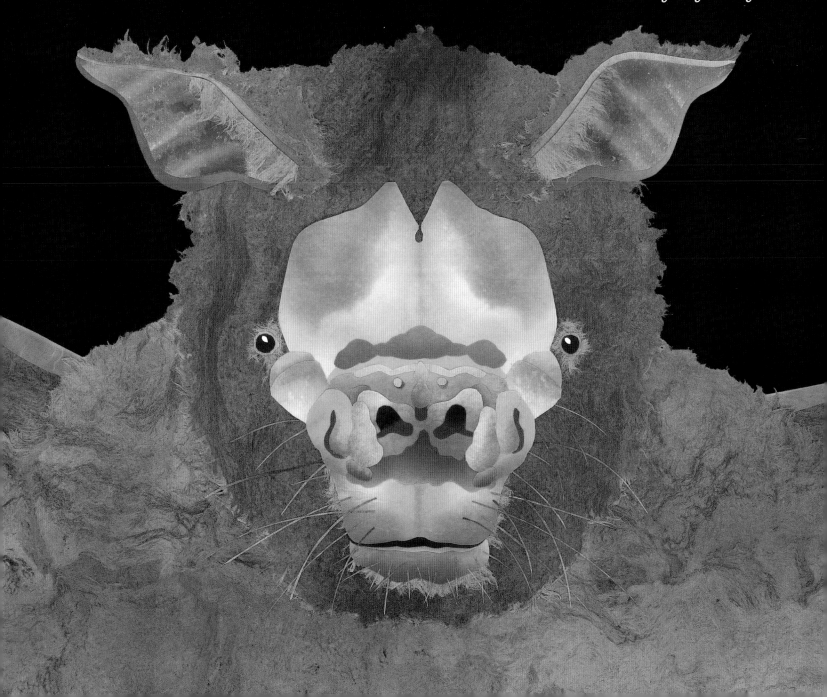

Dear leaf-nosed bat:

Seriously, is that your nose?

I know, I know — it looks strange. But my nose directs the high-pitched sounds I make, which helps me find my way as I fly.

Dear horned frog:

Your mouth is ginormous. Why so big?

Dear frilled lizard:

What are you wearing around your neck?

That's my frill — extra skin that I unfurl when I feel threatened. Pretty scary, isn't it?

Dear mandrill:

Why is your nose
so colorful?

My bright red and
blue nose tells other
mandrills that I'm
a full-grown male
monkey, so they'd
better not mess with
me. My rear end is
pretty colorful too,
but I'd rather not
talk about that.

Dear Egyptian vulture:

Why no feathers on your face?

Are you sure you want to know? Really? Okay, I'll tell you. I stick my face into the bodies of the dead animals I eat, and feathers would get pretty messy . . .

Dear tapir:
Why is your nose crooked?

The tapir has a funny nose. At least, it looks funny to us. To the tapir, however, its nose is not a joke. Being able to twist its snout from side to side helps this plant eater get to food in hard-to-reach places.

Many creatures have a nose, mouth, eyes, feathers, or some other part that looks odd, silly, or even frightening. But these unusual features are there for a reason. In some way, they help these animals survive.

In *Creature Features* we go right to the source and ask twenty-five different animals to explain their strange appearance.

So, what does that tapir have to say for itself?

My nose isn't always twisted. I bend it when I want to reach some tender leaves or fruit.

25
Animals
Explain Why
They Look
the Way
They Do

CREATURE FEATURES

Steve Jenkins & Robin Page

Houghton Mifflin Harcourt · Boston · New York

Well, I like to eat. But I don't have teeth, so I swallow my prey whole. I'll gulp down mice, lizards, spiders, insects — just about anything I can fit into my mouth.

Dear hamster:

Why are your
cheeks so fat?

Hold on. That's not
fat — it's my dinner. I
store seeds and nuts
in my cheeks. I'll
take them back to my
burrow and eat them
later.

**Dear
pufferfish:**
You've got me
worried — are you
going to explode?

No, I won't burst.
I've inflated my body
with water to make it
tougher for a big fish
to swallow me.

**Dear bighorn
sheep:**

Don't those huge
horns get in your
way?

They can be a pain.
But I'm a male sheep,
and to impress females
I have to fight with
other guys. We bang
our heads together,
and my big horns help
me win.

Dear babirusa:
Your tusks look dangerous — do you fight with them?

Sometimes. I battle other males for territory or mates, and it can get pretty rough.

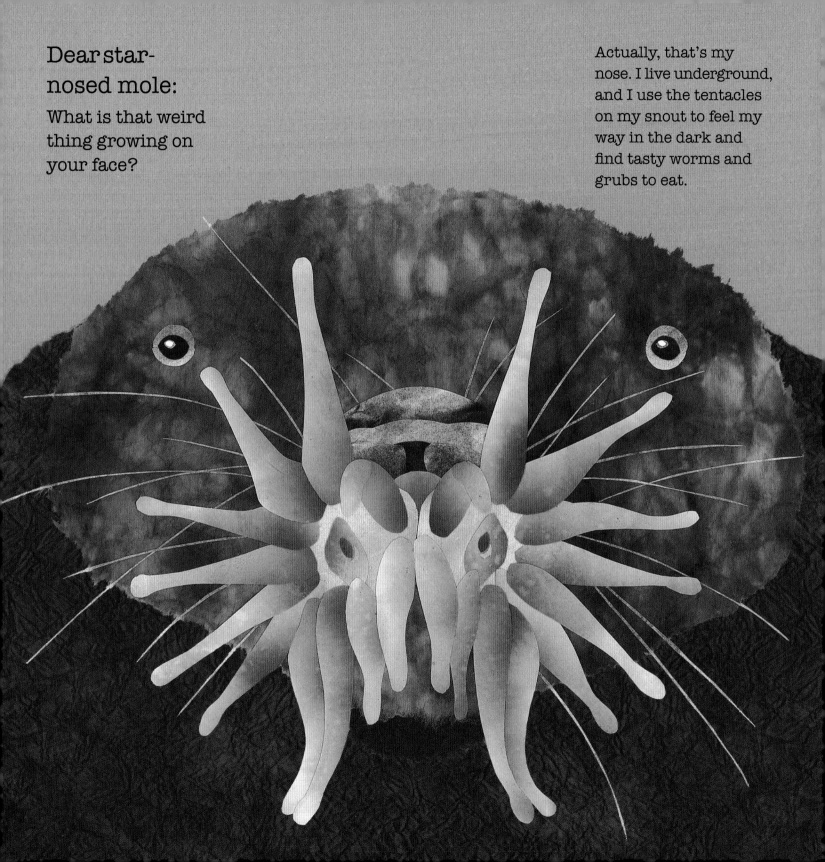

Dear star-nosed mole:
What is that weird thing growing on your face?

Actually, that's my nose. I live underground, and I use the tentacles on my snout to feel my way in the dark and find tasty worms and grubs to eat.

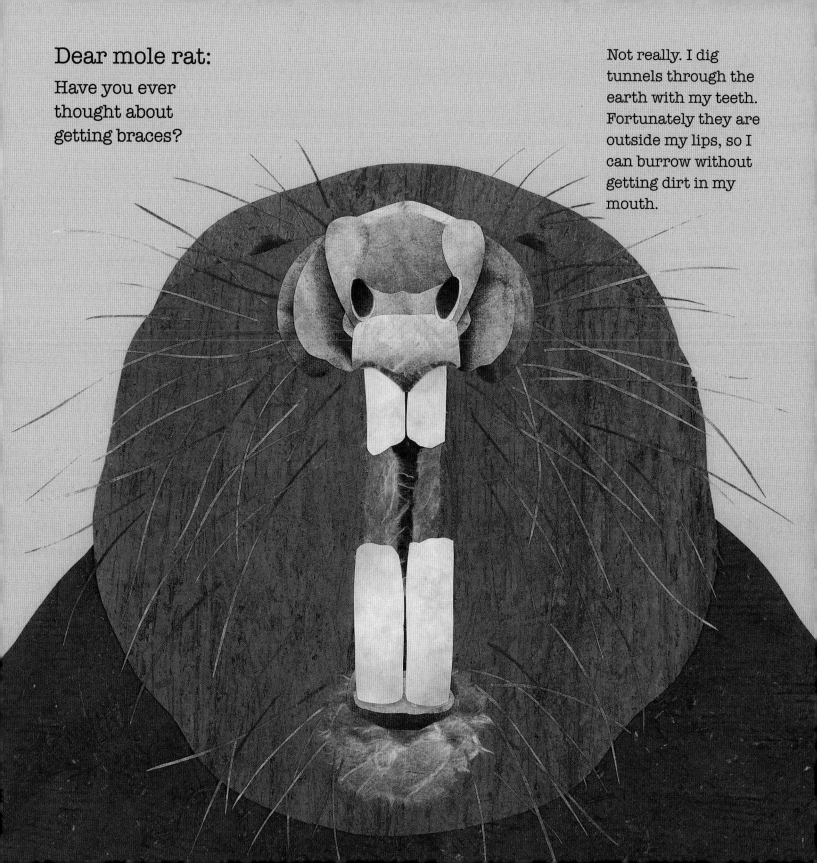

Dear mole rat:

Have you ever
thought about
getting braces?

Not really. I dig
tunnels through the
earth with my teeth.
Fortunately they are
outside my lips, so I
can burrow without
getting dirt in my
mouth.

Dear bearded seal:

Don't those whiskers tickle?

Not that I've noticed. I use them to feel along the sea floor for crabs, clams, and other good things to eat.

Dear axolotl:
Why do you have
feathers growing
out of your head?

Those aren't
feathers — they're
gills. They let me
breathe underwater.
And in case you're
wondering, my
name is pronounced
ak-*suh-lot-ul.*

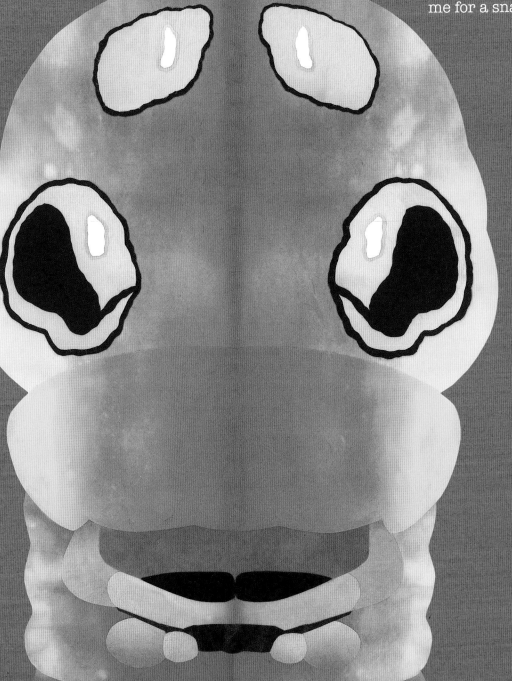

**Dear
spicebush
swallowtail
caterpillar:**

Why are you
staring at me?

Ha! Fooled you.
Those aren't my eyes
— they're spots on
my tail. But hungry
birds leave me alone
because they mistake
me for a snake.

Dear giant panda:

Who gave you those black eyes?

No one. We pandas all have them. The dark fur around my eyes makes me look bigger and fiercer to a predator. I hope.

Dear red squirrel:

Does that fur on your ears help you hear better?

No. It's there to keep my ears warm. It falls off in the summer and grows back in the winter.

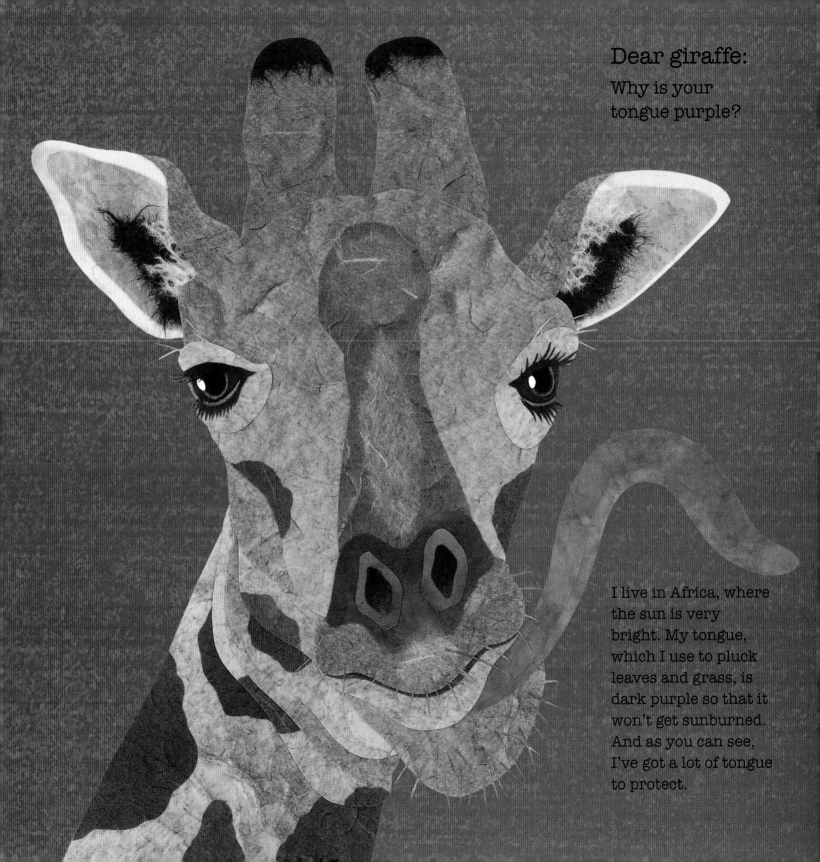

Dear giraffe:

Why is your
tongue purple?

I live in Africa, where
the sun is very
bright. My tongue,
which I use to pluck
leaves and grass, is
dark purple so that it
won't get sunburned.
And as you can see,
I've got a lot of tongue
to protect.

Dear blobfish:

What on earth
happened to you?

Being on dry land — instead of in the ocean — is my problem. At home, deep in the sea, I look like just another fish. But I'm out of the water, and gravity is smushing me. Here's what I usually look like:

Dear sun bear:

Why is your
tongue so long?

I love to eat ants and
termites. With my
long tongue, I can
reach into their nests
and slurp them up.

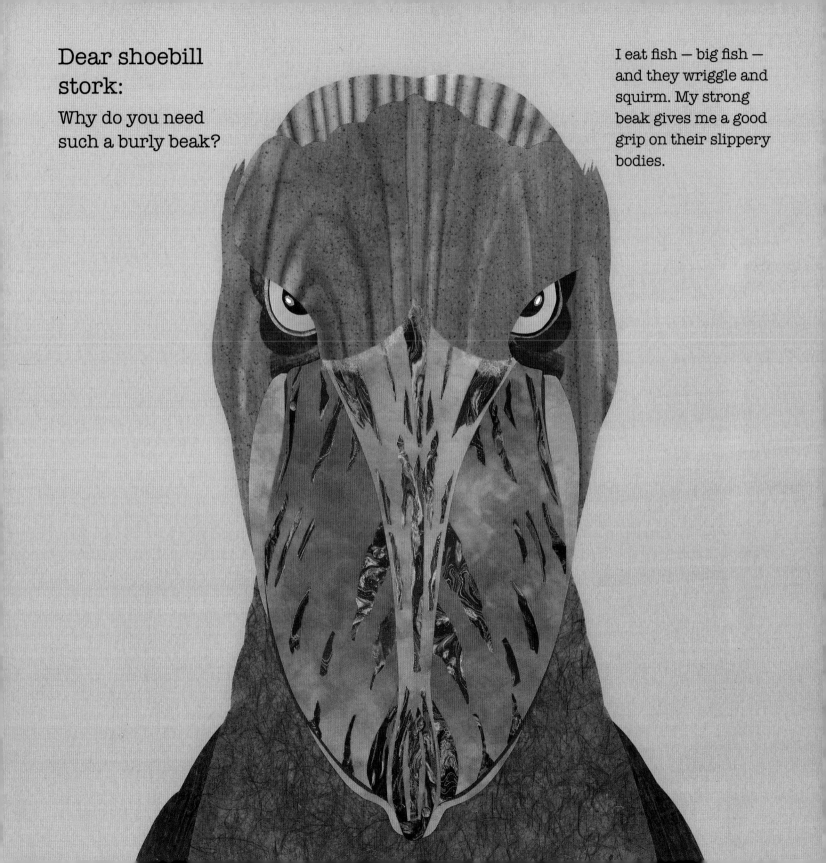

Dear shoebill stork:

Why do you need such a burly beak?

I eat fish — big fish — and they wriggle and squirm. My strong beak gives me a good grip on their slippery bodies.

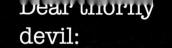
Dear thorny devil:

Why are you so spiny?

Think about it. Would you want to bite down on me? Not many animals would. My spines also direct any rainwater that falls on my head right into my mouth.

And finally, dear rock hyrax, a question for you:

What sharp teeth you have! Are you dangerous?

Not usually — I'm a vegetarian. But I'll defend myself with my tusks if I have to.

Turn the page to learn more about the animals in this book.

tapir

diet: leaves, buds, grass, water plants

mandrill

diet: fruit, seeds, eggs, small animals

red fan parrot

diet: fruit, leaves

leaf-nosed bat

diet: insects

horned frog

diet: insects, reptiles, small rodents

bighorn sheep

diet: grass, leaves, twigs

All of the animals on these two pages — and the adult human above — are shown at the same scale.

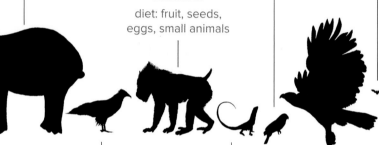

Egyptian vulture

diet: carrion, eggs, small animals

frilled lizard

diet: insects, small animals

harpy eagle

diet: birds, snakes, monkeys, sloths

hamster*

diet: fruit, seeds, insects, carrion

pufferfish

diet: algae, zooplankton

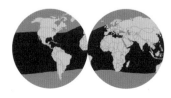

* range of wild population

star-nosed mole

diet: worms, insects, small aquatic animals

spicebush swallowtail

diet: laurel leaves

red squirrel

diet: nuts, seeds, berries, insects

sun bear

diet: fruit, roots, insects, small animals

thorny devil

diet: ants

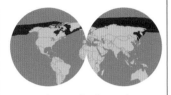

bearded seal

diet: clams, squid, and fish

giant panda

diet: bamboo

babirusa

diet: fruit, leaves, roots

mole rat

diet: tubers, stems, roots

axolotl

diet: worms, insect larvae, small fish

shoebill stork

diet: fish, reptiles, small mammals

giraffe

diet: leaves of trees and shrubs

blobfish

diet: mollusks, crabs, sea urchins

rock hyrax

diet: grasses, leaves, insects, and grubs

For Jamie, Alec, and Page

To learn about the making of this book go to:
stevejenkinsbooks.com/creaturefeatures.

Bibliography

Animal. By James Balog. Graphis Press, 1998.

Animal Fact File. By Dr. Tony Hare. Checkmark Books, 1999.

Animal Life. By Jill Bailey. Oxford University Press, 1994.

Dramatic Displays. By Time Knight. Heinemann Library, 2003.

More Than Human. By Tim Flach. Abrams, 2012.

Smithsonian Natural History. Edited by Kathryn Hennessey.
   Dorling Kindersley, 2010.

The Way Nature Works. Edited by Robin Rees. Macmillan, 1992.

www.hmhco.com

The text of this book is set in American Typewriter Regular and Proxima Nova Regular and Bold.

The illustrations are torn- and cut-paper collage.

Library of Congress Cataloging-in-Publication Data is on file.

ISBN 978-0-544-23351-5

Manufactured in China

SCP 10 9 8 7 6 5 4 3 2 1

4500477991